Liquid love
and other longings
selected poems

Norman G. Kester

DISTRICT SIX PRESS
Toronto, Canada

also by **Norman G. Kester**

Liberating Minds
From here to District Six: a South African memoir

Copy edited by Elizabeth Phinney
Cover art and design by Brian Lam
Graphic design by Ash Kousa
Interior photographs and author photograph by Tania Sanhueza
Printed by Coach House Printing, Toronto
First edition, January 2002

National Library of Canada Cataloguing in Publication Data

Kester, Norman G., 1962,–
Liquid love and other longings: selected poems

ISBN 0-9686342-1-4

I. Title.

PS8571.E785L56 2002   C811'.54 C2001-902328-6
PR9199.3.K277L56 2002

DISTRICT SIX PRESS
c/o 2412-77 Huntley Street, Toronto, Ontario, Canada M4Y 2P3

Writing is an act of desire [and identity], as is reading.

–Dionne Brand, *A Map to the Door of No Return*

they looked to the sea; across the lonely tides
they saw each other always

Poetry always brought him [back to him, to her and] home.

–bell hooks, *Wounds of Passion*

Now that I have declared the foundations
of my love, I surrender this century to you.

–Pablo Neruda, *Cien sonetos de amor
/ One Hundred Love Sonnets*

Love is so powerful, it's like unseen flowers under your
feet as you walk.

–Bessie Head

I paint myself because I am so often alone and because
I am the subject I know best.

–Frida Khalo

For She whose waters gave me Life,
for She who was my first Lover, teacher
and theorist and for those who have
loved me openly, and I them.

Contents

he speaks (and asks questions of himself and his mother/land)

Tell me about what this collection has to do with your mother and love, with desire, even identity?

Well, actually a lot. Whenever, I am about to fall asleep, I speak with my mother, now long departed. Metaphorically, she is both my mentor and tor-mentor. I can speak with her and find ways to create her, but I cannot be with her. It seems a bit mixed up, but through my writing, my life and world become much clearer and so does my missing childhood relationship with her. In essence, this is what the ultimate form of love is. That of the mother's bond with the child and the child with his mother. A bond so significant, it should not be removed. I think that I've held back my love from others too long. My first collection reunited me with my native land, South Africa, my coloured and black culture and with the historical and political circumstances that separated us forever. That is how I came to tell my story. And now, in my wavy words, I am sailing further creatively, to speak about an enduring theme, a theme so universal to the human experience, it cannot be ignored. Love speaks, and I have known its name. It was also my family's shame.

What about the idea of art and being human?

Art is the spiritual practice of being, loving and the interaction with all natural elements: the earth, water, air and fire. As well as how we relate to these. I am referring to such elements in my work in different metaphorical ways. Through story, my poetry has its own unique voice and tends to draw abstract images of liquid, visceral landscapes. Landscapes on which we move through and in— conceptualizing, breathing, swimming, submerging and floating upon freely or transfixing ourselves to another state and to a different place and time. I am also speaking of postcoloniality, of national identity and a crisis in identity and being, too. I can see my coloured (racially mixed), brown and black body doing things, or me saying things that may have universal meaning. We are all too human with many frailties. We battle extremes daily. We are loving, kind, yet at the same time voice anger and feel hatred much like nations. This kind of ambiguity is seen in my art and my humanity.

Is art "love"?

Yes, very much so! Some artists may not agree with me. However, how can something that is created with the heart and the hands, that comes from one's deepest core, not be part of love and that which is to represent humanity? Art is a conscious or subconscious representation of love or different themes of love, loss, desire and death. And one's racial and gendered identity. The brushstrokes we make, the pot we've shaped delicately with our hands, fingers and thumbs, are but a gesture of love. Art, or the making of art, is the process of giving in or letting go totally. The ability to create, to become, to live fully and existentially is to know one's self, the world and its constant unfolding. The artist surrenders herself to herself, her work and love again and again. Painfully, beautifully. That is the artistic life. That is art's true purpose.

You were going to include the word "betrayal" in the book's title...

I thought I might, but then I didn't. My creative work should speak for itself. I believe that betrayal—the ultimate form of the absence of trust, the ultimate death in the pursuit of friendship and love—is a concept so powerful it cannot be put on the page or painted. To some degree, I have felt as though my mother was the ultimate victim of betrayal. My sisters understand this, too. Many in society have known this, not just my family. It is handed down from generation to generation, from family member to family member and from parent to child. Nations betray their own citizens, and they also betray other nations. Ethnic and religious conflict comes quickly. Look at South Africa, India and the ongoing bloody conflict between Israel and the Palestinians and the fires that have raged endlessly in the Middle East.

One of the greatest examples of betrayal is the enslavement of over one hundred million Africans and the destruction of Africa's families, culture and civilization. This, based merely on the colour of one's skin as was the case in South Africa. Slavery produced generations who suffered severe oppression. It separated and destroyed families and even today we are left with its disastrous consequences. The American Dream is but a figment of the imagination, both democratically and socio-politically. It is a nation filled with shame, attempting to give love. Yet it still takes it away. Death row is the result of America's violent rage on black men, and the violent deaths of black men in Toronto have remained unsolved for too long. The black community has rightfully laid blame on an unrelentless government led by Premier Harris that has drastically cut welfare and social housing. This has hurt our families and life. Can we say Canada has loved more? Look at its treatment of First Nations peoples. Look at what Toronto Mayor Mel Lastman said about Africans—that they are "natives" to be feared, that they would put him "in a pot of boiling water and dance around him"—and the white Canadian-controlled media chose to ignore the racist dimensions of his remarks only to examine the fact that the mayor's comments could cause the loss of the next Olympic bid! We've been betrayed by a white culture that does not understand us, that continues to renunciate our cultural being through colonization and false or negated images of our identity within the white-controlled mass media.

Then again, perhaps I should ask myself if I am making too many assumptions on the basis of where I come from. Has apartheid made me too blind or unwilling to let go of my biases against white domination and capitalism? To some degree, perhaps I have also failed to live ethically so this is a betrayal of self, of self-love. Yet I feel bound to my mother culture and *not* to Canada. Readers and various critics of my work may think otherwise.

You sound angry.

That is what is said of black men and our creative or intellectual work. We deconstruct and sometimes self-destruct, voicing our rage, speaking loudly. The latter is very African. It is always part of who we are and that which we create. Anger comes from society's castration of our manhood, our body, our masculinity and even our love. Anger is the unconsoled black mother who is raped by white society, by both white and black men, and anger is also the mother who mourns for her children removed to another country, taken from her. They may be in another land, but they still reach out for one another, hoping to meet again.

Who influenced you and your work? How is this revealed?

I'd say my ancestors, my living with my father and sisters, and without my mother. Knowing them. Realizing who I am as an artist now after the death of my parents and my new life with my sisters. And of course, coming from such a strange yet beautiful place as South Africa with all of its racial strife. If you look at my creative work, I sometimes take an autobiographical idea, philosophize about its meaning and then mix it with cultural, religious and other references. This becomes art. Black writing stems from our family world, our connection with the land and sea and from our oppression and liberation. For this work, I have looked to many love poets including Pablo Neruda, ntozake shange, Federico Garcia Lorca, Mexican nationalist and painter Frida Khalo, Bessie Head and other writers. And furthermore, I cannot forget the brave and beautiful words of Dionne Brand. Memory, love's loss and its divine madness have also propelled me to a large extent. And then I have constantly listened to the sound of the sea, to the languish of love music from the ages, including jazz singers such as Sarah Vaughan, Nina Simone and Molly Johnson. Black theatre, film and cultural studies have also made my pen work, and photographs and paintings have also revealed a certain hidden truth about life. I sometimes become the photographer and ethnographer, even the painter and subject.

What are you looking for in life and in your work?

Like anyone in this century of hope, I am searching for meaning, for a deeper relationship with the earth and for love of some sort. And to a great extent, if you come across my pages in this collection, you'll see what I mean, what I am attempting to understand or portray.

What then is the meaning of poetry and even your life?

To allow people, either those who love me or my readers, to experience me fully, nakedly through *story*. I could be a woman, the budding leaves of a tree, or something mellifluous such as the sea or an innocent child. Then I have to ask myself, do I make a distinction between myself and my art and/or me? I don't think so unless the piece paints an image that is largely about something or someone outside of myself, but it still has meaning for my world and work. The artist cannot escape herself even if she creates other wor(l)ds. Her work is a subconscious portrayal of her life or parts of her life, touched by a thousand hands. Poetry is painting words on the page and it *is* performance. It is also about saying, seeing and sensing something so beautiful, or ugly, it cannot be ignored. Poetry is artful loving and loving art. Like other forms of art, poetry is about creating, seeing, shaping, touching and sensing. Poetry is work because it speaks so beautifully. To cry, to die with each stroke, one must look and repaint images many times over until the beauty of perfection occurs. It comes from the core, from the heart, from *all* of us. It takes everything out of you and makes you think of life and love.

Why has poetry come to you now? What do you think of the events of September 11, 2001?

Because I am growing and experiencing change and have the desire to recreate myself after so much tragedy. My life has now come full circle with the death of my parents and with my three sisters and myself wanting so much more in life. Pablo Neruda's work has touched me deeply, here. He too wrote of and by the sea. Many people don't know that water is the most *yin* of the elements and that it also relates to our dark and not only our soft, feminine side. Water is cooling and relaxing, yet forceful. It brought us to new lands far away from home, and it functions as a mental and psychological gateway of yearning to that time, place and space. The middle passage, the brutal and cosmic causeway to our diasporic identity and culture. Neruda's incredible and lifetime artistic work says something so deeply personal about life and, indeed, love and humanity. Yet he suffered deeply from the political climate of the time, too.

If my first literary work—*From here to District Six: a South African memoir*—was about home and identity and renaming myself as an African, I have thought that it is love, it is the simple art of poetry, that I am now seeking to find, to refine. All writing is really history. *And, poetry is the heart and art of language and love.* Yet love and loss are interchangeable in life and in South Africa. They have meant the same thing to coloured and black African families who have lost so much due to apartheid. Universally, black love and family life are essentially about loss—the stuff of history, philosophy and fiction. And black love is revolutionary: it is power and poetry.

Now in this century we are looking for much more, yet desire to live simple lives despite the advent of technology. Westernization has speeded up life and social chaos and economic inequality have increased. Culture is globalized *not* localized. The unexpected bombing of the World Trade Center by a number of Muslim terrorists, the loss of innocent lives and the direct consequences that led to President Bush's declaration that his administration would now focus on eradicating terrorism throughout the world pose a serious threat to world peace. A vulnerable America now seeks vengeance since its heart and its centre of capitalism have been bombed. Arabs, even Islam, are now looked upon as "evil," the new evil that America wants to destroy and obliterate. And those nations suspected of harbouring the so-called "terrorists" are to be run out of business by America and indeed invaded if necessary. It startles the imagination to hear of this and to see various citizens agreeing to this kind of war rhetoric without asking the real motive behind such governmental actions.

The American media that gave its unequivocal support to the Vietnam War in a much earlier time have implied that "terrorists" could be your next-door neighbours and they could certainly be those opposed to the American government. Dissent therefore seemed futile as far-reaching and questionable legislation has been quickly passed by world governments. A chilling atmosphere of arrest and detention without due process and guilt by association has come about with the imposition of "heightened security" measures that severely restrict freedom of speech, the freedom of the press, the freedom of movement and access to information, thus posing a grave threat to fundamental civil liberties. Premier Harris, whose political life was at stake, told Ontarians that his government would ensure a restricted and tighter border relating to immigrants who posed any threat to Canada's national security, despite this being a federal area of jurisdiction. Associating new immigrants and refugees with terrorism was the provincial government's new answer to the nation's grave concerns. It was its new battlefront and political weapon targeting ethnic minorities, filling the air with racist undertones.

In a much early time, American intelligence and financial aid had initially supported the *mujahedeen* in fending off Russia, and it helped to bring about the obliteration and destruction of an already war-torn Afghanistan and its rich culture. And later, neighbouring Pakistan gave rise to an extreme ruling Taliban and its militant Islamic army with the aid of wealthy, anti-Western and formerly CIA-trained Osama bin Laden whose Al Queda network may have helped to ignite the explosive and ripple-like events and after-effects of September 11, 2001. The world has changed radically in a few weeks. Yet in the end, people wait for bread and love—*not* vengeful bombs of mass destruction, not an appeasement of food aid by which the U.S. hopes to win over its coalition members despite its aerial war that has displaced millions. The enemy is now within the psyche of the American mind. Metaphorically, it *is* the American mind.

President Bush asked the plausible question on a televised address to his nation: "How could they [the terrorists and the Middle East] hate America so much?". Americans do not fully understand or realize that throughout America's imperialist history, their nation had either invaded liberated countries or soon backed oppressive military regimes that had quelled dissent and freedom, especially in the Middle East. As reported in *NOW Magazine* (October 11:19), National Board of Peace Action member Rahul Mahajan and Dr. Robert Jensen of the University of Texas have thought that the "US wants to dictate the manner in which [oil] wells and pipelines are developed in Central Asia for its own and American corporations' interests." Bin Laden has become a side issue yet a much demonized figure in the American mind, though the President used him as he pleased to seek America's misguided revenge and to score politically with his public and his political rivals. This new century was to be filled with hope and peace, not war. America and its allies have sorely let the world down by making us feel terribly afraid, rather than asking why the events of September 11 happened. Of course the taking of civilian lives by terrorists should not be forgotten, but neither should acts of ignominious war and the state slaughtering innocent lives. People who have only known war and hunger. Where will it all end?

And finally, where do you think this book will take you?

Simply put, to leaving the past behind. For most post-colonial writers, the past, present and future are connected as one moving and vibrant stream as it forms our consciousness and world and writing. There is no separation. For myself, in order to mature creatively, in order to find a space and place that is finally home, I think this book—save for my memoir—is about finding this. And in a sense I am saying to myself, it is time to move on, to no longer live *without* my mother. That whatever happened was but a part of the tragic tide of history. That South Africa fondly remembers her children. That love exists as the universal potential to find nurturing and move beyond racism, brutality, colonialism, xenophobia, genocide and even war.

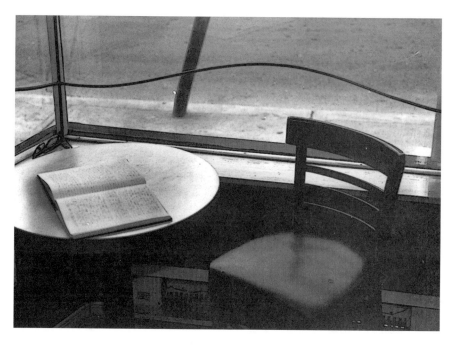

storms / seeds

the ocean took him there

one cannot theorize and speak of love
or study it from the dusty pages of
history, lights on; the library of life is
quiet and staid; one must live love, feel its
mysterious breath and passionate, dark pain
its desirous depth, misery and even madness.

the flower petal asks the blue bird

if
the body
prepares
for death—and it does

does
it also
prepare
for life, for love?

yes.
it opens
up
and
begins
to let
go
of fear.

it heals.

it seeks
forgiveness.

it relinquishes
all
control
and
power

and
finally
sings
away
shame,
and
guilt

it flows, becomes...

he hears rhymes

"i thought i'd
lose all of
my sexual power
if i had
sex
but i didn't
i still read
their palms," he says, miraculously

staring out at me
over pasta, he takes my potter's hand
and caresses it with his own
bruised with
the ugliness of life, longing for love

the small island's
men are
friends to their
wives, and they
sometimes have
men ... only a few are known to be that way

winged like a black dove,
lush, lovely and magical
she came to him
waves, words, wisdom
and all of her naked, beautiful breath

gently, to his warm bed
he took her words that could not easily be bought
his mouth no longer spoke
intellectually as a man uttering false truths
as a man who was once accused
of stealing and buying women's innocence
betrayal is man and man is betrayal
thought and spoke she

how he wanted to take her by
her calm sea, to hear the wind's secret whispers
like her delicate hand as it painted the land's summery kisses
to see the island's sun set, hand held in warm hand
pages and pages like endless tides covering
and keeping them both safe
from the vicissitudes and viciousness of war.

torn love, lost innocence

he comes
intimately close
like
hot black blood
mixing with
hot black blood
then
quickly shies
away, hides
his love
and manhood
like a mischievous
little seven-year-old
running
back to his
safe haven of dreams
—a quiet, solitary hell
as if he
wants to escape
only to come
back
as a close, dear friend
who once betrayed
his hurt lover
in the end

he could let the world down
but he knows how to
make love to strangers

the market and its fruit

Kensington is filled with smiles and sorrow, with life and pain. It is a metaphor for living, for grieving. I am the vegetable gardener, the homeless woman who mumbles to herself and asks for pennies, not smiles, that will feed her this morning. See the manic painter who does not sleep, who dreams in bright red, blue and black, muddy unknown waters painting his toes? I, too, am he. And the lonely middle-aged wife who picks up lettuce from the old box, feeling each for their worth. My unsure hands are her kind ones. She, the one who looks European, who has lived overseas without her husband and four children, now holds three yellow lemons close to her bruised heart as she pays for them. I am also the black woman who walks slowly, slowly pushing her cart in her festive Sunday hat. Orange and mango-green signs across the dirty road leading the way. I am the eleven-year-old daughter in a yellow pullover showing her mother to the smoked fish store with fresh loaves of bread stacked high in the window. Stories of sumptuous specials.

The grey-bearded poet who left America, America the home of two people, two myths, two secrets, love and death, dreams and tragedy, looks at a passerby while speaking to one of his friends. I am he and I am the tall, black muscled man who brings fresh fruit and fish—smells of yesterday—to the market each morning. He sailed here searching for home as did my father. And I am also the sun that calls out slowly today, rising slowly, clouds moving out, urgent hope coming alive ever so briefly, my body warming to its child's gentle touch.

My soul waits for word, for whispers of wild love.

waves / amor

love rains on me
soothingly
the sea, *our* sea
is your moist dark hair
like seaweed, braided and thick
my painter's hand glides right
through its silky sand
these soft black rivers flow
over my man-child's body
naked, brown and warm
to the touch, you write your
painful story all over me, and i you

teeth pulling up on fleshy gold nipples, hard
through your midnight-black nylon net bra
my firm bloodied thing
is a playful veiny paddle
soon searching
for your liquid, fuzzy
dark warmth wanting me
...a heavenly smile from you
your lips, the sea
your lips, the sea
cunt crazy
eyes closed, eyes closed
and quietly, unexpectedly
—*une petite mort*

libraries and intercourse

the man who looked at her from afar
from time to time now kissed her
wildly, his soft
hot lips lingering
on sweet petals
the taste of fresh banana bread
pages covering them like wet rainy sheets
hearts pumping, hearts racing
his kind hands pulled her into him
and he into her frail, fatherless body
her delicate hands as beautiful as her breezy brown eyes
she didn't want to hear
that he had kissed a young man
she only smiled to tell him
of her first time
an embarrassed moment, flowers
flaming red shirt on his tight shaven chest
and against the small of her covered young breasts
breasts like the woman he hadn't seen
that weaned a sleepless child
breasts that were yearned for
to touch, taste, tongue
the steel door opened quickly
they walked out like a loyal team
yet with guilty smiles turning
to 9-5 boredom and suburban suicide
skies blue and even dark grey
with life opened as wide as the sea's depth
golden sunsets, hazy full moons leading them home
he pushed his thing into his pants
after it sprung up excitedly like spring's joy
and then an empty pen was taken up
to help someone find
a book on dating rituals in africa

she who has died a thousand times too many, who lost her heart
wears only bitterness and sorrow yet does not see love speaking to her

he lines up and jives with the regent park boys, aged ten

"tell me about love," he asks them shyly, and they
three culprits, friends, homeboys
smile, smile with each other and smile,
big, big, beach ball aside, coloured with silky dirt and play
"if we do, can we bud in front of you, huh?"
say they, all three, unsuredly
black, white and black
they like to shoot hoops though the brothas' bullets pass their way
yet today they three wait anxiously in line
for the coool poool
twenty-four hot degrees in heat
a blonde baby boy runs, smilin round buggin dem

...ok
they three sing:
luv is
beautiful
peaceful
lovin with all hearts
nothin more than love
it's—i love you!
it's wonderful
it has a sexy body!
pretty
sexy
sexy is nasty!
he's a sexpot!
give me a *patwa* word...
i was born here, one of dem says
love is
marriage
and buried at peace
...i don't know no more

and so they quickly bud in line in front of him, bashfully and he eyes them later jumpin
in de poool, slidin down de waddah slide: laughin, runnin, hoppin
into a field of flowers so blinding bright, so dreamy blue, he cannot paint it

the journey

prime beef cuts / the old portuguese butcher sits and eats calmly / in his small shop / salted fish from home / leads them to this picturesque island / dusty underwood / scriptor smells like 1976 / nadia does her splits on the black and white / roasted curry spices / sunflower yellow / ethiopia comes alive / sandblasted washed low-rise denims / that will tightly hug slim hips above hairless studded navels and cracked leather jackets / hang cheaply outside with life / as they shop smilingly / the summer is wild with sexy sun, rain and full moons / he sneezes again / stevie wonder echoes, "my cherie amour" a few quick doors down / she likes the cool adidas runners / afroed roberta lived / in a phone booth for a dressing room / the girl's tryin to make the world real, fight war / when she sings love, "we are in love" / "her words are conscious music—togetherness," / says the brotha in sun-yellow turtleneck / he always smiles lusciously at the shy love-child / not expecting anything much in return / baby-blue roller skates, an old funky orange plastic phone, a black disco turn table and lp's / memories of living / in housing that weeps inside on orpington / daddy locks out two spirited girls in thick black platforms / at the stroke of midnight with a broomstick / spanish vibes now make him dance / naked / THIS AIN'T NO GAP AD reads a homemade sign inside funky astro / "yeah, burgundy n' russian red lips are in big-time," says the man who wears purple fish-eyed glasses, like a seventies idol / the grandson of the famous woman *griotte* / "men who talk to garbage cans and ride junk bikes own buildings here," he smiles / the poet pussy-kisses her after coffee and love poems, coffee and love poems / holding warm wrinkled hands / they two from the mainland rock gently like waves from their old creaky porch painted / maroon red / and speak of lotuses and in tongues from a distant time and place

the spirit god of man

i am only her plaything despite my hardness
mother nature, her goddess groove always rules
father is phallos yet missing
his silent ways, always unknown
i pray that he does not enter
into my gloomy room when we fuck
i am Her, with shaven balls
that hang lifelessly and expose
themselves to ridicule as they
pop out embarrassingly, hairlessly, shiningly
i am Her, waiting and standing
up, up, upright—
helmeted, shaven and ready
thick-veined, my ejaculation
is an incredible story, a super surge
pierced, ringed, tattooed, i am worshipped by
men who walk quickly on dark, lonely streets
in japan i am a revered tree
in christianity i am the enemy: satan
i am *lingam* in the *yoni*
i live for my man's hard, veiny firmness
not my softness or gentle touch
at midlife the penis ponders, with too many thoughts
and desires a return to adolescent days of raging hard erections
when i enter her—she helps me like a child, slowly, slowly in, out and in
i am the soaring skyscraper in the city; she, the opening silky dome,
with life's sensual liquid light, calling me, calling me in heat
i am the seed of knowledge, the tree, the artist's mad, red brushstrokes
when i leave, i die, millions of my tiny, white leaves
are sprinkled quickly, swimmingly in her warm womanly river
and only one is needed as she throws away the rest
my man's thing becomes just a plaything—
brown, beheaded, shrivelled.

the voyage of the kajama

the creaking of the three masts, masts that once sailed the high seas, as a north wind breeze rises onboard beautifully: "i was made for the sea," says she rather slowly, sipping red wine; brown, brown hair blowing like a daughter of the warm wind, eyes wonder and wait; photographs become soft smiles, tenderness, memory; "water's me, water's me," i hear again as my painter's eye captures her sea, her silent calm; thoughts of him in and out, in and out of her, swelling from loving, and then he drifted away like a distant seafaring stranger; at dinner with the wind howling she looked too frail, cigarette held pensively, eyes reciting a poem and pain penned madly in love with her blood, eyes too crazy to see the truth; he left her adrift and shipwrecked; the silver of the moon looks down high above before sunset and she laughs like the waves, she laughs like the waves wickedly and wildly; our hearts, silent like the sea and wind is she, wind is she; the yin-yang of life as the black of an empty cargo ship passes us by and the heavy concrete heat of the city is now miles out, lives and decades away; helplessly, the island reaches its young hands out to us, the sails blowing full out.

rope burns on my singing palms, rope burns on my mourning palms as i run to pull the sails down; hairy bare legs and brown feet steadying on the slippery deck; arms working ruggedly, hands working quickly, eyes waiting for signals from the crew; wind as hard as thunder blowing us down, nearly blowing the mainmast and distant city down; booms of thunder as far and as dark as the swirling blue-black clouds above, as near as lightning's white cold, bold kiss; the storm, we think, has passed, the waves have slowly soothed, too unexpectedly; strong hands, strong hands, though we are all too afraid, too uncertain; calm but dark, calm but dark and the sea's mist surrounds us; like children in a pool, we stare out into the vast void and depth; eyes afraid, hands holding rails; shades of sea from tropical green to blue to mossy black; hundreds of sea birds circle eerily in the early night sky; then, rain as thick as snow and pouring like showering sheets, sheets showering; a stirring of the waves, viciously.

enraged, her water breaks unforgivingly as the deckmen work and run madly; excited cries mix with showers and showers and showers turning to love raining down, turning to love raining down; passengers are buried in the hatch below; talk of messed-up lives—women and men; above, wet bare chests and fragile sunburnt bodies wrestle to brave the sea's roughness, her wind and stormy rains; soaked, he comes to her gently like a god crying out in the night; he excites her, incites her and touches her; sweet-talks between biting kisses and licks; black silk negligee now ripped off to quell her heat, she wraps her long hungry legs around him fiercely: she has always loved him like cuba; months later and aboard the deck, life and death have passed and we look to the sea—still black waters surround us; caressingly and fatherly i hold her simply like her only son who was once lost; my dark brown eyes are ablaze at the sea's unknown ease and she looks out at her years and lives of living; love is missing yet her lonely womb is now set free.

man sitting and talking

we ride endlessly back to the city
of lost souls and sunny bicycle rides where
people live in expensive skyhigh boxes
he speaks of friends stricken ill, snow-haired like him
his sweet hands have nursed me from love wounds
too deep to heal and i along with him
have seen ten years too many
go by, passing us like seasons, seconds
in words, wine and wisdom
"zucchinis were the first to grow in my
father's garden in brandon," says he rather fondly
and i wish my father were here to see him and me
as close as father and son, as friends who grieve not, but live
aches and pains between laughter and his cast of funny characters
like my father, i write tearful letters of love home
life in the dark of night stares quietly at us from outside
and we two do not know where the empty bumpy bus will let us off

the body and bread of christ

he lies there, his beautiful head
thinking bloody things
it was his mother who last packed his
lunch that day with the last of
the bread to touch his hungry lips
yet she only saw him on television
with no knowledge that one bullet
had pierced his angry head full of hair
and the other his celestial soul
fires raged on hot city streets that day
as feet ran down genoa's cobblestone roads
as gas drew tears and water pushed
the people back, not bringing them forth

red flowers now lay close to his silent heart
his gravestone is but a torn piece of paper
held up by a teargas canister, blowing
in the crying wind.

adam n' eve: niggers of america

getting
and eating
pussy
was love
he thought and
wanting pussy was
how women
wanted to
be known, licked
heard, looked at
he thought
pussy juice
talked more
than pricks
brothas
blk coons
like him
only darker
the honey-coloured
dread-locked
woman
actor
he met
slapped his
brain silly
one night
"honey, i ain't no bitch" she scoffed
"wash yo mouth n'
head out
'for u come jive
with me that way!"

he went back to his books
even eldridge cleaver
n' malcolm
said the sistah
got a point: now don't
u be datin no white
gal who'll u
get more 'spect from
u'll cook n' she'll pay
the goddamn rent!

momma came into his
dark room one night
where she saw him ballin
"child," she said
after hearin his story,
"take the hand of that
gentle island woman
mend your hurtin ways
hug her like god, like love
she ain't no master's
house slave that's been done
gone to bed with him
for centuries
unloved, thrown out
she got a beautiful mind n' heart
she's   *us*
all body/blood/sweat/soul n' tears
she's everything ... the Dream
she's our people
our praises ... our words."

the blood of the angry earth

Rain bled from the angry earth for days, for nights, at the place where two shining
towers burned majestically, the place where their gold was made though the world
still starved silently without rice. Dust came, like a yellow storm exploding with

falling debris and the putrid smell of death. They could only save a few and a
multitude of body bags went back soulless. I finally put down my pondering pen
to spill contempt for a nation still in mourning. Anger turns to sadness, anger

turns to burning flags and to speaking softly to my neighbour. Two close sisters
tried calling each other while screaming flames trapped them, while all around
their world came to a crying halt and a short man in a tight expensive suit speaks

in two tongues because his heart is filled with vengeful rage and his mind only
thinks of terror, of war and guns, as he sits calmly in a garden of blue roses. His
nation bears its mourning flags from every post, its people cry like children who

have lost their only dream and my mother puts her arm around me as if to say
they who have been kissed by Death now also shed tears. Everyone speaks quietly
and in the same way, everyone with a pale face now thinks evil mad thoughts of

those in cream-coloured saris and angry blue turbans and mosques have barbed wire
erected around them. Imams pray for peace and unity while a man condemned and
hunted by the infidels who were blind to the hunger and savage slaughter of

millions waits for word from high above. Poetry is forbidden. Children eat mulberries,
their stomachs empty like hidden caves. Black bombs bombard Kabul nightly,
bombs of destruction followed by bales of blood-soaked food falling from the sky.

Innocence and guilt are but one as are love and hatred. The Arabian Peninsula
flows with unsuspecting quick winds of change as the anxious feet of the invaders
defile land most holy. Nothing, only a few buds, grow on steep snowy mountains

where they will soon fight, where blood will spill like seed, where metal and might
and the earth's fury will petrify all. Money and power are worthless now. All I have
are unsold words. My books are stacked high with dusty age. "Let's go out," says my

best friend who loves me quietly, and I quickly call my sisters to calm their fear, to
see if they are all right, to see if we are still alive with the quiet beauty of life.

15

a recent photograph of the artist

breathlessly
nightly and
in vain
he searched
for her
and for him
it was the
category of "other"
that attracted his
inquisitive, deep
shy eyes
for it was in
that space and time
where he looked
for familiarity,
for home and love.

frida y yo (frida and i)

your deep dark eyes
the delicate hue of my mother's praying hands
caress me, hold and enthrall me
i want to taste your soft painful lips
the colour of the earth, the people's life blood
lips that cried, lips like night's lonely tides
                              your beautiful body
                              crushed, but not lost, like mine
                              desiring love, feeling betrayed
                              monkeys guard and whisper to you
                              cacti, birds of paradise and deer
                              surround us, our desire, our people
your young breasts, pinned paintings
that fed mexico are my mother's that
could not nurture us, a nation in mourning
wombless, you could not bear a child
and i could not guide a son's gentle hand
                              we smile as children play, laughingly
                              in the dusty hot street near your home
                              your *padre* photographed and my father could
                              only paint his life, loveless and silent
                              your heavy dark eyebrows become distant rivers
yet i want to swim them and hold your soft arm
that glides through water, sunny eyes seeing
the ache of history, hands speaking of life's stories
—pain, pleasure, perfection
pricked by tortured branches, piercing hearts
                              is it i whom you dream of, young frida?
                              listen to the parrots that call out my name
                              weave your spider's web, think not of him
                              let me unwrap your dark rivers of long black hair
                              that embrace and strangle your wounded self
where are my mother's blood-red dresses
and her cherished wedding ring?
my man's hands crave to loosen the strings
of your pleated tehuana skirt, pleadingly
yet your eyes say no *gracias*, no *gracias*,
                              instead we dance, twisted bodies touching lightly
                              like sea to shore, our gentle hands hold brushes
                              of red anguish delicately, painting each other
                              if only for one day, one night, for one final sitting.

sonnet XXIV

Of all the moons that came to me, falling
in oceans, rivers, streams
I desired only one, one
I have since left this life, for love.

Of all the tides, one after one, hurtling to shore
bringing sand, wood, bottles and messages of hope
I desired only one my wave, one my love—
the naked tide of your being, your warm body.

Your tears, your branches and seeds
all grow now in my garden of earthly desire:
they bring me rain and quench my thirst.

I desire only to touch your potter's hands. They are the people.
Your mother is the beautiful *Isla Mujera* and your father is strong like the sea.
My last poem will be written about you and it will be for love, only love.

tides / memories

I am

black
the colour
of my country's pain
its dark stories—the rape of women, land and children

brown, coloured
the nation's soul, its tender but scattered soil
rivers of sorrow flowing to her stormy sea
rivers of diamonds flowing to her calm sea

ochre red
black and white:
beads worn gracefully
as gifts of love.

fire and ice

his body burned so much on fire that he dove in from sandy shallow to neck-deep
underwater, seeing only soft sand and a forgotten tire, as time remembers
stroking dark brown arms madly, heaving hot shaven chest
heart beating furiously, heart racing like her hot mind
and flicking his legs fast, mouth and eyes closed tightly
the journey out to africa through foggy, freezing waters
that were once thick with ice through clouds of algae
is unknown and perilous   facing skyward   up, up, back
as he looks to sky blue and hot sun glaring at him like a child of the sea
in the glow of her vast warmness, he comes dripping naked
sun on him, sun around him, damp feathers now washed ashore
sea-smooth stones now washed ashore
memories, distant; love, adrift yet as beautiful and as sandy as a smiling breeze
holding you like god; wave upon wave of dandelion breaths
call out to him, encircling around him, taking him, taking the centuries of heat,
and his body as it flowed slowly, slowly to shrinking shore.

one day in a lifetime

waves wash forth / passing time, passing bodies / the boy runs naked and wildly
through flaming sun and sand / as if school is already out / tides long in the dead
heat / tides of foreign perspiring bodies / laying, waiting, watching / for word of
their future / what will it bring, mean / the breeze, its summery feel is my life /
alone, i stand and question the distant shore, search for clues, calm dreams and
precious stones that i take home with me like my sisters' wanting hands holding
mine / gentle yet hard and wet to the touch, they strip me bare of the city's cold
concrete polluted ways / i am naked if only for one day / my body blazes brazilian
brown quickly and wet with dark desirous beauty.

waters tell secrets

i missed him as much
as stroking my tanned
dancer's arms through
my mother's watery hair

crying out with loneliness
i noticed for the first time
in a long while that the soft,
brown hair on my courageous chest

had sprouted as if to call me
knowing for once that his
quick absence or the push
of my arm against his

boyish man's chest would
close me off again, close me off again
and rip the sea's silent breath,
its life and young heart from me

all at once

daddy shouts "you're no son of mine!" and i retreat again silently, witheringly

she asks if he will see the full moon tonight

will you come
with me by my sea?
i usually live
there alone...
the moon
will be full and shining
with a silver lining
exploding with starry-eyed
kisses in the dark of night

deep currents

i am black but not
yet desire to love someone black
yet can i take his or her hand
the dark image of s/he
i have been taught and
told not to by my country
and father—but why do i want to return home?

su cara (his face)

in his face, smiling yet unsure
i saw me,
brown, sad south african eyes
wearing years of lost innocence
i painted myself in his youth
the sea took him quietly
and he became its unending rhythm
it became him—love
and i swam hurriedly to
his safe shore, his being
to run like the tides
weeping, blossoming

this solitary breath

this gentle grass, flowing like endless ocean currents
encircling, adoring him
this young tree, yet named
this innocent young flower—rouge red, soft, soft, wet petals, still silently in bloom
wanting sweet caresses, *bisos*
rain, flowing rain, kisses and kisses of soft rain

this unknown man painting himself
without any adornments or that gold gucci necklace
that was given to him by his first
the world waits before him
searching, soulfully seeking like his people—still
the young woman whose flesh he craved, caressed, she now gone
the child, a son, hers forever
that adoring, excitable and screaming son
an enraged young man
seeking a father who ran away,
seeking wisdom like his island's sun

this grasping hand, like the child's
that held a rose, breathing fresh new life, a whisper turning to love
close to your open heart, that stroked a pen's ink
turning to black blood   blood of africa, bleeding
this hand that gave comfort to deep painful wounds
unhealed, bloodied by time
this arm, that pushed away men's angry words as if they were biting bullets,
this delicate brown neck, holding a head
held high and full of dreamy wor(l)ds
floating, flying back, flying, flying back in time

to zulu mines and eland dances, curries, biltong,
springbok springing skyward across dusty open velds
to mine-dumps tall as mountains
tall as skyscrapers towering overhead
this body, so old and young it
still retains memories of pain and pleasure
adventure and excitement
of distant places, places distant
beaches, beautiful words, passionate words like diamonds discovered in river beds
smiling sunsets and long, stretching
bare beaches that held no laughter or life until africa smiled for a moment
ocean currents, green with envy lick you
away—always, sway you back, forth, back, forth
these small brown feet
that pounded down heavy pavements, across endless countrysides, up steep hills
the endless track of Life, waitin
runnin, sprintin, searching life a lost nigga without a home

breathless
breathless, still breathless with salty sweat
these sinewy legs that jumped across stormy sands
like daddy as a young man in the cape   he eyes her, she smiles at him shyly
he calls him to his room to take naps, to fondly nurture him like she would have
and bogart's toughness in black and white romances both of them, only to leave
her voiceless

these innocent eyes that had seen all yet nothing
open ears that remembered fond, funny stories, wanting more
these soft brown eyes that had cried at night's end as
tearful whispers to her were still of all three of them,
the fragile earth's starving, homeless children
recantings of dreams, hopes, illusions, passions
he was the eldest yet the youngest
the unconsoled father and lost son, the mother, the sister, brother, trickster,
trancer and confidant

these words uttered from a silent mouth: these sensuous lips
wanting soft, sweet caresses
a beautiful mouth that laughed, smiled, yawned, scorned and pondered
this fragile earth
this mythical land he remembered, yearned and returned to
her unclothed body held high by coloured sisters of god, daughters of africa
her lone body placed in the curry-red earth, scattered rose petals, rain, hymns,
endless tears
as he turned to an innocent, naughty boy who nearly burned half the house down
as he ripped himself apart over and over again

this desperate earth
beckoning, calling, crying, remembering
this free yet chained land, this abandoned people, this life, this brave and exhausted
body that swayed to rhythmic waves and was nudged by naked, invisible bodies,
wet with thirst
that moved alone in the dark to slow unsmiling beats
brown eyes closed, hands and arms pushing away heat, searching in the smoky air
feet beat to black beat
they drinkin, lookin, wantin
faces painted by deep, fiery rivers of pain
           feet beat to black beat   beat to black beat
                  his heart beats   to black beat
                        his heart beats   to black beat
                              beats to black beat   beats to black beat

the son speaks as his father slowly sleeps forever

my bleeding pen writes with rage, rage and fear
paints strange, pretty pictures i could never show you
i spoke about my life yet you were silent, angry with me
there were too many of them calling the lonely apartment

who were these blaady people, you wondered
"*boetie*, here's the car for tennis—be back early"
i took it gladly, and then when he was in his drunken sleep,
i'd leave a small silent note, to pick up the keys, tiptoeing

out the heavy door to escape like a freed nigger, speed downtown
at night to see friends and dance with the jamaican who would
return home one day, who would want to be with his wife and son again
life was too complicated; men leave they do not love; my eyes are blinded by whiteness

he, the miner, makes himself another sad long drink, just vodka no milk
the television is left on for hours, the *star* in hand, and he dreams of rugby
but there is no real conversation between father and son, father and daughters
i was crying out wordlessly like a mute blind child, searching hopelessly

love spoke to us yet you did not carry its winged message; you cried over
and over again, fatherless, motherless and without a wife's warm, smiling ways
but we were too young to hold you or you did not allow us to as time tried to heal
the deep, bloody wounds that could not be washed clean of the old country—mummy

and a lonely nation scarred and still at war with the colour black

we were mixed/up, thinking, not acting white/right

i have waited too long

i have waited too long
for love
its tender, fragrant touch
and gentle feel
do not come my way
there may be smiles, smoky wet kisses in the dark
but mostly strange, distant looks
junk e-mail comes my way, not love notes or bouquets

i have waited too long
for love
the road to being two
instead of one
is mountainous
freedom comes with a price tag
freedom comes with quick death
gasping for home, for sunny shores
grey wet snow buries
my secluded desire
deep, deep, deeper

i have waited too long
for love
my people know this too
she, the motherless child who bore me
he, the spoiled mine painter who fathered me
and my ancient strong sisters
three mysterious flames, africa mourning
love is lost
to white asylums and blank stares outside of dim hospital rooms
to electric shocks to the brain that are promised as love letters
love waits alone like a beaten coloured woman at an empty train station
her son left unnursed

the beauty of the longest day

for once i am silent and your delicate body
speaks only to me; my storm of moist kisses
are not yet fully planted on your smooth, misty neck
your english is less than perfect but everything that is you
is like the seductive sweetness of your lips, the scent of wild
rose petals in early june smelling like love
i could not paint the soft shapely slope
of your young womanhood, your face is both exile and another
country; we were not yet properly introduced
(what would your father think of me?)
i remember the shy of your small breasts speaking through
the tight white of your thin t-shirt—veiled, unexplored territory

                    your dark eyes looked strikingly at me when we
                    first saw each other at the pool's edge and then
                    you made me my favourite hot meal; my weak
                    asian eyes trailed you, my desirous whispers
                    followed you, craved for you; i had the nerve to
                    say "oh yes, i'm painting love—will you sit for me?"
                    my canvas was bare before i met you and then
                    a full gentle smile from your blossomy lips
                    hidden thoughts from me on how it would be to curl
                    up with you as a vainless lion to an untamed river
                    to be with you, arms full and warm, to silently
                    mouth, *je t'aime, je t'aime...*

a deeper shade of black

The drums beat and beat and beat. They are feverish. A muggy, breezy day. A different rhythmic beat comes through the air. An incredible surge of excitement stirs. Why has this place, this market space become so symbolic, so joyous yet mysterious to me? Kensington is a meeting place of many different worlds, both old and new, fragmented and whole. Spiritual. Lovers drink rich, hot black coffee cheaply in love and it reminds me of the black seductress' run-down voice. The drums rise again, and with each different beat this place lives, and every new day is a new story with a different meaning, the old one colliding with the new. Every generation comes here; they and their children. And the beats picks up again. Rise. Rise. Pulse. And fade out. And out a number of people assemble to look, take heed. Pay attention to its memory, healing. Drums heal; they speak, even tremble, and make you think. Home calls only to those who let the drums come to them openly and freely like a beating meditation, a story of love for the land, the sea and the people. I paint its meaning again and again. I am the outcast, the black sun, the missing brother, Africa listening, longing. I move and dance to what I hear. The open sky is not smiling blue and the sun is left to mourn and cry. And the drums speak again. The drums speak again, make love. And the drummers gather together, their beat rolls, comes through the air, drifting towards me, slowly, louder, slowly, faster again and again—and I breathe, think. Only here do I breathe.

the child cries out the answer

and when i stuck my head underneath
the sink's tap, eyes closed, eyes afraid
i believed you'd cut it off, again
the executioner's shining blade dripping fresh
with my innocent boy's blood, the faggot in me
finally killed and stomped out by the lynch mob
dragging me to the awaiting bridge (or did they
want to take me to the old oak tree?)

the preacher spat on me and read from his *bible*
savagely; the white children were hoisted high on
their fathers' guilty shoulders to see the nigger burn
"burn nigger burn!" they shouted and prayed, smiling
smelling my scarred, ripped torn flesh; my niggered
and powerful delicate thing they have feared breathlessly
for centuries cut off, choking my dry, flaming and tender throat

the crowd stood still silently, finally, blue eyes shining
with boyish innocence and rapture; then they gathered
to have a church picnic to exchange parts of me as lovely gifts

*father forgive him, father forgive them, for they do not
know what they do*

a virgin, asleep

she lays there quietly, there in the sun
like an innocent woman who has never
tasted the love of a young man
waiting for me to undo her easily untied yellow troubles
she does not recognize me, small chest breathing
panting up, down, up, down
young, not yet ripe breasts, not yet teethed by a baby
closed, closed, pretty protea soft eyes
hiding her sweet oily musk underneath tiny slivers of cotton
a flat, hairless tummy, a soft and exotic navel, springlike in smell
exposed and touched only by sun, water, wind, rain and the softness of innocent hands
the mouth of the blue sky opens with smiles
a sea, a sea and a homeless people
and greek ships called our *oupas*, and my dark *ouma* washed on st. helena
and english gentlemen's hands asked delicate yet poor coloured hands to dance, there
she turns this way, sees the sea behind her only to find none of her friends there
and her girlishly slim shoulders are silent now, waiting
my bushman's body yearns for her secretly still even though i am old and nameless
she lays back, back to take another few seconds of sinful sun
before a year of blizzards, before school
the leaves have fallen too early
the leaves have fallen too early
they are golden yellow, bright orange unexpected, exploding reminders
yet she blooms quickly like any child of the earth
her face is that of a nubile virgin
she will wear see-through white, unsplashed by blood and bathe
in rose-water before her wedding night
she and young her lover will take the garden route and go to the sea and speak
her soft, round lips are mine unspoken and i search vainlessly like an ex-boyfriend
wishing to call

rain plummets sorrowfully like love

my heart bleeds pain like the cut of a knife
cold, callous and castratingly
through me   i hear your voice
it is mournful, soft
calling me witheringly
the sun does not shine today, but
my outside plants have now all flowered
they, all three, my sisters—africa
are lively and pink, the promise
of unexpected snow
covering my hand's beautiful blood
madness is but a cruel joke
and life's punishment
—poverty grows, not love

i live to see your beautiful, quiet eyes, *ja*
they always caressed me and remind me
of her loneliness, her brutalized garden
as cold rains fell like her moods to give way to calm
the mist descended slowly from the mountains onto
the sea like death calling
my sunburnt arms, the drunken sins of my father
the curse of my family and history's wrongs
follow me to my grave and my
ma who lost her ma early whispers to me as i sleep
and dream of dark blue skies, the hot veld, our memory
drifting lonely as driftwood from sea to shore
my lips cry to her like her doting little *boetie*.
"i have always loved you and i have never left you
you are forever in my mind, and i am forever your son."

liefdesgedig / love poem

the heart cannot lie
it only knows
and dies of sweet sorrow

blessed are those
who find and feel
love for it is noble

and it is the water
of life, the pulse
of mankind, the

milk that feeds
our children from
our mothers' breasts

the memories that
my mouth mourns musically
comes from my people

the land is my hot country,
and the place i will lay to rest
is the cool sea, taking me

to my mother's warm arms
—she no longer walks the
streets alone, waiting.

untitled, hanlan's beach, toronto, 7.10.2000

I.

he thought of him like a young black rose at the sea
a shudder sublime of insecurity and suspicion
and the sea, like a mirror sparkled, calling them both
but black ears are deaf to the laughter of water
the freedom of waves, the flow of swooshing sound knows their name
and distant drums beat, the hot island and coloured people calling them
both, one—a fuchsia flower in his fro, the other, a flower on his lips
both—leafless *griots*, but boys waiting in dark alleys for nameless men
who will call them onward home, who will plant seeds
on their gut, who will send them baggageless to momma
a ladybug bit one on the back, a brown seed fell on the other's dark lap, and
they two did speak of guilt, shame, grief and sorrow
in muted tones cuz he has torn the tongue
out of the other's mouth and the other bleeds for water
warm waters surrounded them both, its warm, warm mother's belly keeping them safe
from men's angry fists and phalluses; this is the fortitude of black love, the twilight of skin

II.

the sand is hot like hell, the leaves tell rhyming stories that they know, understand, recognize
where not to fall but to embrace both she and he, he and she
the *loquats* are nastier on her tongue than his, but the kiss is always sweeter
and she makes sweet *koeksisters* on sundays for all of them, even for those living next door
her tears are the strains of boiled cod and the madhouse in benoni she lived in
was both her home and prison, her exile and tearful escape of dark anguish
under which she bloomed and bathed, "skin sheds easier with insanity" but hearts
remember partings, beatings and men as they took her and took her, like a nation bearing arms
her womb was displaced and strung up to decorate their empty walls
to hang bushy-headed embryos in oils not yet dry, a boil waiting to burst
a lone flower soon bloomed in a field where she laid to rest; it was young and picking it,
she grew it as one of her own, watering it to remind her of holding him, to soothe widowhood.

This poem was composed with poet andra simons.

he returns to his fantasy lover every night after dinner

dark haired and
dark flaming eyes
he makes love to women
he hardly even knows
desirous looks
thirsty images
and glistening brown breasts
nipples of innocent lost desire
nipples of dark, sensuous desire
mummy called
him like a giggly girl
of seventeen
to the desirous screen
and he returned
to her every night
passionately
like a faithful lover
bearing fresh flowers of joy

south africa, mon amour

they think the good *kaffir*
is the "yes *baas*!" of yesterday
and the bad *kaffir* is the "no white man!" of today
but where is the coloured man?
does he still sit on the fence of life
watching history go by to repeat itself
or is this place too black for him now
to see himself reflected here?
is this africa, is this africa
with aids babies who cry blindly and die nightly
without their mothers, without their mother's warm milk?
is this his nation's new apartheid
is this freedom, the new renaissance
is this africa, is this africa
is this love calling like the sea's constant longing for home
our people's name betrayed and ashamed?

that day there, amongst the crowd

That day there, amongst the crowd they walked.
That day there, amongst the crowd they walked and talked.
That day there, amongst the crowd they walked and talked. It was hot. And they ate spicy samoosas. Drank freshly squeezed orange and strawberry juice. "You know we're part Greek," she said sleepily. And he agreed, looking at his dark brown skin that glistened like gold. They packed up the wet towel they sat on and continued through the slow-moving people.

That day there, amongst the crowd they walked. It was hot. Then they sat and she ordered a coffee. He asked for bottled water. The bill came to $5.50 without a tip. A smoke came in between quick sips, in between frightened hands and small conversation. They sat with men who were noisy, rough and said "ain't" a lot. Who seemed to know everyone, here.

That day there, amongst the crowd they walked back. It was hot. A small, sweet Greek donut like *koeksisters* came next. And then they ate a bit of curried Chinese noodles for $3.00. He fed her some, using his lonely fork. She took a gentle bite. Then he quickly ate the rest.

That day there, amongst the crowd they walked further back towards his old bicycle, now locked. The music was loud. People were leaving the streets. Then she said she had something to tell him. He took her to a café and listened in between quick gulps of cold apple juice, holding out his hand, which she took as tears came down her brown pale face. "I miss her. Sometimes I think I should be all black or all white." Silence. The sun streamed through open windows; they sat quietly, tiredly. He noticed a slim young man writing, sitting close by.

That day there, after walking through the crowd, he went into a bookstore that he hadn't noticed before. She came with. She stood close by, then browsed the children's section, before going outside for a smoke. He quickly flipped through pages of a book and bought it written by a black woman instead of taking the love poetry of a white woman who killed herself. It was cheaper but worth more.

At the corner before leaving each other, she hugged him as hard as an expensive diamond, unable to let go. He stayed in her worn, motherly arms, feeling alone, as if he were swimming by himself in an empty cool pool.

the birthday brunch

my hair grows like seaweed, she smiles
strands become stories
stories turning into thorny necklaces around her throat
she casually glances at her mother who wants to see her funky new purse
eyes filled with loneliness, her mother looks to her for reassurance
and wants to remember the beauty of her young childhood
days of diapers and daughterly playfulness
when smiles and laughter filled their place
now, hungry for a hug, starved for love
she realizes that the lingering aroma of curry she cooked no longer fills the condo
as polish food doesn't need spice, the fatherless father of their young daughter says
hungry for a hug, starved for love
her mother weeps inside like the nation that bore her

sisters of the distant earth

i scour the bare earth
their brave cries for home
to see the velds, smell and
eat savoury curries smilingly,
their lone children's voices
and distant telephone calls
made silent by endless memories
of mummy's lone, beating heart heard
over and over again, even still now
like dead carcasses i thought they would
forever choke me but i touch them
all three, really all four, every single
hundred of them
alive for once, no thrice and they
smile, smile, smile
laugh out loud, as loud as the sun's hot hand above,
as loud as the moon's smile beyond and that
is all i ever wanted them to feel, to be, to *love*.

joy

they three once dressed the same now want something new of life
after their infertile gardens have remained barren for too long
flowers need watering as much as abandoned women need love
one is happily back with her first, the other polishes grimy tubs with
beautiful hands and sings simple songs while the third lives comfortably sleeping early
the youngest and only niece wants to fit into a skimpy string bikini for miami
and now i see it is time for me to slowly let go of them while i nurture a child yet born
a child with the rarest of names called Love, while a woman whose hands speak
softly though more than my lips, may soon meet mine with life and home

karaoke song

i am the sea; your shore guides me and only in the secret intimacy of night's stillness
can these words be said to you and now i realize that these stars above are our children
the sea's sounds are the blue of waves sweeping over our voices, bodies, hands and feet
hearts waking from the exhaustion of heat as illusion turns to laughter
you're vulnerable to lies like the beautiful things your hands make
i touched your long, winding hair as if it were gold, as it blew in the wind yesterday
and when we spoke you asked my name; secret smiles and talking over
homemade steak pie under trees fanning our lives and childish ways,
a plastic fork turns the sweet dark icing of your chunky chocolate cake into waves of
mountains from the southwest—curves, colours—the stuff of o'keefe not khalo;
that was yesterday and tonight i wonder, waiting for your surprising return
my rosy pen is hurrying to hide before you see me nervous and too naked.

the beach

like the taste of sweet chocolate condoms, her mouthful of kisses were remembered most
/ all raindrops, all secret wet kisses / as if the day's angry heat had given way to love raining
down on us, caressing our sweat-filled, muddy bodies / standing in the gentle lip of the
silent cool sea, she stripped down shyly to her slinky white bikini bottom and me to my
cotton briefs / a kiss from me on her silky neck / and then she kissed my searing
tattooed heart that no one else had touched—"oh, it tastes like rain," i heard from her
soft, secret lips / my brave writing hand held her close to me and then love-bites on her
milky ripe nipples, ripe as the sweet, red apple we both fed on later / eyes wide, eyes
surprised / a quick toss of her flimsy black bra to the soft sand to let go of all else as
showery rain fell from above to quench the heat's hunger and our own / we were all
smiles, all incredible joyous smiles as two laughed as one, as two laughed as one.

small bits of wood near my shore

he was living like she, in isolation
minds, bodies, drifting apart
minds, bodies, floating apart
but thinking the same

mi amor holds me under the deep
current, head resting on my shore
always, always

i read these wurds to you
as they are my flesh and blood
i read these wurds to you
as they are my flesh and blood

our desperate lived lives were
mummy's sacrifice and freedom
her love and betrayal

love's face was absent
yet it wanted to become them
her lace outfits
and prized ribboned hats
to protect her mind from the
madness of the sun
were gone, as were her
table cloth, now washed
upon the cold, polluted shores
where he swam and painted

life is many frayed
pieces of withered rope
rope that shaking hands cannot tie
rope hanging loosely from my old shorts
that cannot be pulled up on my blk body
i am naked and the world is dressed

she walks like a european
tryin to fit in; they spit in her steps
she walks like european
only black hot inside, only black hot inside

he lived in small places high above
in the sky where books soon outnumbered
men and words of passion became his
domain and endless ocean

he believed his poetry would bring her
and him back to love, back to he
who wrote and asked unanswered questions

poetry is desire and prayer
poetry is desire and prayer
pain left his body and empty world

her coloured womb is a place
i bury my self
i paint my self
as a spoiled, sorrowful
and unloved child
...suffering—poetry, is love

he gave his close three
used books disguised as love
and tosses out the nation's ideas, words
their empire: white, strong, and fucking free
and replaces them with
the hidden truth and memory
of his people and people's people
the deep deepness and arduous longing
of his blk blood
wurd by wurd, day by day and hand by hand

he could not have those whose seed gave him a resonant voice / they died too young /
too guilty with time and space / the torrential storms of time interrupted their far journey
apart / those wanting sex / looked only at his elegant paintings / not at his strangely
coloured body / or his weak asian eyes

39

the father, the son and holy ghost

No. I have not seen him for some time, the man.
No. I have not heard his lonely voice. Smoking. Thinking.
Another love letter to his sister. Blonde-haired ladies whom he dated and who
like ballet, wait unloved. Our voices are not the same, yet they speak the same.
God, he looks. God he looks at us, silently as the man. He saves us from this life.
His cross is put on my forehead—for love, yet I do not remember feeling the pain
or noticing it. At age two, her mother died from a head injury. And a million miles
from home, I feel it.

The creator is here. Like the lost people, he guides me. Like the lost people,
he meets me at the Cape, and Dr. Abduraham is there and my father and uncle
speak to him as inquisitive boys. I join the darkies at the Coon Carnival who sing
their moppies, yet they love their English songs more. The whites laugh at us and
use their own amenities, which are cleaned. A Coon captain visits the Star cinema in
District Six every Friday just to get new ideas for the carnival. The father meets me on
Hanover Street, and is seen in the face of a homeless woman, my mother's age. Both
hold out hands for water and pennies, for love and mercy.

He, the father, must have smiled and jumped for joy as well as drank with the boys
at the Kemo Hotel when he knew his first and only son was born. The last child.
Yet it only meant another coloured. What did he say to his wife, our mother who
prayed on the blood-soaked straw in the stable, and where were my sisters? Did
they bring water to bathe me from the well? Our well of hope and utter despair.

Did he know I would speak of him this way? Did he know I would imagine him,
paint him, pray for him? Attempt to portray who he is, and in becoming him, I had
to leave him behind. I had to leave, to finally find and be with Her. Yet my return
would be different, joyous, yet different.

I wonder what the father would have thought of me writing daily, bringing in the flock
from their lonely, hot fields? I wonder what the father would have thought
of me speaking of him like this, so openly, so bravely? "But *boetie*, you will live
a solitary life of longing," he said, when I told him of my secret love.

Like father, like son, I am him, simply. I am him, strong, resilient finding my shattered
voice on this hard earth, this cold, desperate land and planet, the beckoning sea calling
us, guiding us. And I am also Her gently, gently holding us together as one people,
scribbling out and feeling our lost language, our *meaning*. As one people.

the day trudeau died (le jours où trudeau est mort)

mummy,

> trudeau died today.
> shubha called to tell me as she drove around aimlessly, thinking alone. and
> i weeped for you and daddy, and i weeped for you and daddy, red cheeks
> and all, as the television blared, with moments of his glory playing of the
> man who had never even thought of the trappings of power. oh, but how
> he danced, did pirouettes and poses in front of the television for us. he
> quoted plato and visited the people of castro, china and russia, dislikingly
> watched by the elephant that grunted. girls screamed candescently for him
> to kiss them like elvis. he stood his ground on st. jean baptiste day, glass
> bottles flying around at him, the police beating up angry mobs, mobs
> becoming flq cells, naming themselves *les nègres blancs d'amérique—les terroristes*
> *québécois*, later exploding bombs, kidnapping and killing. lévesque's angry
> children who would plot and kill, who disliked but loved him. the runaway
> child of the nation does not mourn but scorns and revolts, scorns and revolts.

mummy,

> trudeau died today.
> and i fed a cold, weary man on the street with a loonie, then went to buy some
> groceries and fresh, sweet apples, red ones like the colour of the big rose p.e.t.
> wore on his right flat lapel, like daddy, close to his sacred heart, close to
> canada's strong yet unsure heart. the man of ideas asked the world for
> peace, a just society—even love and latin america and the caribbean shook
> hands with trudeau's nation, while the president's men looked the other
> way. and at the store, i eyed a greek woman wearing black hugging her cold
> body, aged with time and eyes never leaving the black and white as she sat
> there quietly. it was as if one of her family had died, like you, like you again
> and again, mummy. "he had such eyes and he has young sons and i'm sorry
> for that," she said softly as i knew her smile often. but today there was none,
> just blank stares and a troubled look, just blank stares and a troubled look.

he speaks softly to her every night in his sleep

deep down, inside me mummy
i want to meet a woman
of black, graceful beauty
i am not afraid to love her
nor to give her dark chocolates—all of me
or sweet, blissful kisses
or hugs of joy
but i am afraid of hurting her
to hold her bravely
but not to share her pain
all of it, all bloody years of it
or tell her of my affection for you
and my sisters—separate seeds needing soft warmth
but afraid of being insensitive
and wounding her
i am not afraid to love her purple seasons, finally
or to know of her people
and their people
or to tell her the truth of our people
and our mournful centuries, the scars of a nation
but afraid that she might reject me
for i have also loved a man, mummy

        that does not mean
        i do not speak to my father
        for he is silent
        and i hear him always
        like the wind rustling the sleeping
        maple trees
        at the black of midnight

a love letter to my son

I write to you from a distant time and place you only vaguely remember my son. *Ja*, the sun shelters me just as it has been following you like the moon as a loving brother, as you have thirsted for my nurturing waters. And I have always felt your ocean. You are forever in my dreams of longing: your tides curl up to me and they flow constantly this way to my sea of despair. This place has changed, yet our people, many gone to distant places, still remain unsettled and without hope. *Without home.* Without all four of you. Africa is still in my blood and her people now rule despite our history's uncertainty. I understand that you want to fall in love with this warm, gentle woman who has lived long. You must hold her delicately, just as you did when we strolled down the streets familiar to me, with children looking at us strangely but fondly. How unusual it was to be with you after our interminable separation, our endless heartache. With you in my arms, I remembered everything as if it were yesterday, and you, wanting to learn about your naughty childhood. The games we played. The songs I sang to you. I told you of those dear, wonderful times. Times of love and pain. Duty and obligation.

I want you to always know my name, my son. Remember me in your daily prayers. Remember me and know that God is with you, as he was with me. Keep counsel over my daughters' affairs for they need a guiding light. An angel. You are their spirit and they are your blood. Guard their secrets as your own; be the gentle hand that protects their innocent flame. Become an affectionate teacher and love my only grand-daughter as your own child. It is she who needs a mother and a father and a family to nurture her as a young woman and daughter of the earth. Speak to her in gentle, funny ways. Remember Daddy too even though it is hard to talk to him. Love your wife if you have her. Listen openly always. If you do not have a wife, you must find one as if you are looking for God. Written with liveliness and youth, your overseas letters tell me that maybe you will always desire to know the language of love.

Do not linger in shame and self-doubt. Free your mind of all worries. Call distant lovers and friends and tell them you miss them. Love also the sick and the aged and the homeless for they need your spirit and mind as you gave them so unwillingly to me. Visit your church and hold hands with the congregation. Read from your *Bible* whatever it may be. Maybe you will do so when you see my small prayer book. I kept it with me despite the sun, rain, dust and the cold winds. Finally, my child, learn from the world. Go out and visit its many people who speak one language. That of peace, not war, reconciliation and justice. They are our neighbours. They will come to you for help, as you did, me. And finally, our people will call upon you one day. That will be the time to leave for home, to speak.

I will forever be here for you—*here* where your heart and mind rest, *here* where you seek sunny contentment and joy instead of pain. Remember to bring fresh cream cake, cool sea water and garlands of Cape flowers if you see me, my son. Come, dress my bare wounds and heart with your fragrant, tender words.

amor perdido (lost love)

i carry my mother's lonely heart
and my nation's eternal pain
all, all fathomless years of it
all, all mournful blue blue tides
sweeping over my fiery brown body
and twisted, broken spine as driftwood floats away
to lost seas of time
to lost seas of time

i carry my mother's lonely heart
and my nation's eternal pain
life's sandy shore, life's eternal voice and calling
are distant yet i hear my people still
waves come and go, waves come and go
i have told her that i will put up a gravestone
on the hot, curry-red earth that nestles her strong body
so close to mine

pools of desire

i am   *deep*
like my mother's ocean—her brave body
of black water escaping me, haunting me
i try to find her beautifully
as i swim gently, to take her liquid, cold touch
in my bruised hands,
to cleanse my brown, bilious body
sometimes i come to her furiously
as she calls me like a young, nubile lover
to save her, to be and speak with her
children play smilingly by her
they love the water as mother is near
they call out, laugh and squirm delightfully
i watch them always and my hand holds their
playful, wet excited hands: they are me at age seven
tears cannot contain me, tears cannot contain me
my brown-haired skin is deathly dry
like the bleachy colour of hard chlorine

the visit

all of his silent life, he missed
his impoverished but loving family
and mother
the nation
and coloured people
mourning their long absence
he missed his father's loneliness
his sisters' friendly
manner and smiles
madness soon disappeared
if only for one day
"it's not your fault,"
he said to her fatherly on the phone
as soft tears ran down her cheek, again
his written words, his languishing books
dusty with the love of scribbling
notes to himself in deep, deep sleep
seemed inconsequent
seemed a secondary thought
and unimportant, now
life came back
to him
like a giant, unstoppable wave
like an ocean
bearing peaceful news
tides of love
and warm condolences
made his cheeks sparkling red
with joy
this is what life
should have been
might have become

love and guilt

he was just seven and i was twenty-four; he was just a boy and i was a young man
in love finding mummy again; he was shy as me, with a dog, yet bonzo's love was missed
he was brown and beautiful, smiling, quiet and naughty like me and today i see

he is bright man: tall, polite and charming
i think he looks up to me; he has brought his mother here finally
he has brought his mother here finally; maybe that is what i should have done

her tears continued to fall unheard over the rough, vast sea
now we meet, now we meet; the cold winds blow, the cold winds blow
i think of her and two of them who live in houses that chain them in fear, to sleep

the third, frightened, restless who cannot dream; i weep for her, for all of them
i soon fell for him, not head over heels; his soft brown eyes glanced at me as we played
our boyish brown bodies lay close on my empty bed and i think he felt a soft

unknown caress; the young woman he met in church, she was still on his quick mind
strange things happen to distant coloured cousins who dream they are in love, who
dream they will lie with each other wordlessly; mothers might weep, mothers might

weep—the congregation will whisper—after all, they prayed together; their breasts
fed sons like the hungry earth; the nation of beautiful exile they come from knows
them all too well; one is free and prospering the other is not, so he paints without

brushes or canvas; one wants only to visit his mother's grave and stay, yet the other
doesn't have the time to throw flowers on his father's empty grave; so the story does
not end here, and so it begins here; kissing cousins, kissing cousins

"i think i just want simplicity," says the older one; "well i'm a perfectionist," says the
other as they have hot *rooibos* tea; smiles over snaps of sunny home

earth, sea

the breast of the earth
was my mother
and her breath was our watery womb
her children, rivers of blood
were nursed by her starved body
washed out to sea
the dry, hot veld is now her gentle lover
brittle bones buried by centuries of longing
her nation no longer at war
mine-dumps overhead
like miles of impassable mountains
alone, i stood at her unmarked grave,
and closed her soft, gentle brown eyes looking through me
heart aching, waters flowing
my tender hands
weeping, no longer painting

man holding young roses

i finally left my mother's arms
and jumped into
a beckoning, warm sea
of forgiveness
its urging more pressing
with every beat of my
fearless, anguished heart
with every step of
the new world that called
me, green with envy
filled with hope
and unexpected love
burning like an unquenchable
fiery, new flame

rain / hands

The tarot reader

I swam to Montreal like a shark to find the man who had watched me closely but quietly on that lively beach. Moons and moons and the distant tides of love had passed us by it seemed. I searched in familiar cafés and restaurants, even Mañana, the Mexican restaurant in the village where we had dined, savouring the same rich, spicy dishes that both of us had shared in Puerto Vallarta, near the sea. Frida Khalo, in one of her striking portraits and probably painted by a local artist, stared out at me painfully and alluringly from her pensive eyes. I took several mental pictures of each place in the city, some by the old port and water, others in the village, so that they could linger longer in my mind. Stay with me forever like the touch of *mi amor*'s tasty lips on mine after sunset. There was even that bride dancing in the street happily with her groom on cobblestone roads as tourists smiled along with them. "You will find pure love and you will also know world fame as an artist—maybe even as a painter," the tarot card reader, dressed in an old pair of faded jeans and sitting in St. Louis Square, told me in her thick accent the next day as I listened intently. So she asked me to choose my seven cards as we sat on an old bench overlooking a magical fountain. "Seven's my lucky number," I said exasperatingly. Going to a tarot reader was never done purposefully by me. It was by mere chance. The last time I had my cards read, I was strolling down on the boardwalk in Toronto, near the beaches, the water and sun and I was simply told "you need to make yourself a home." And I still haven't done it entirely. But is home really *here*? Is home *here...*

Across the road, soft romantic music emanated from one of the old low-rise apartments with its unique iron spiral staircase. It was passionate music that nearly made tears fall freely. I wanted to remember Montreal for its passion—passion to live, to feel, to know love. *Oui.*

the old poet meets the young playwright

He looked
at his delicate, right Hand.
The one he wrote with
its many soft, deep
rivers of pain and insecurity,
and dark unknowingness
and finally decided it was
time to clean his
small, dusty place.

Scattered
with his many
unfinished love poems and
stories of burden, he
would plant
the fruitful Seeds filled with Memory
and distant cries
his Mother had
sent him from her sunny asylum.

Cape gooseberries grew wildly in his prized garden.
There, he and the woman without paper
wrote their many stories as her young son
played. He would try to walk in her fateful footsteps.
Overlooking the concrete world
where two baby seagulls
were born, they two lovers unwrapped
each other's surprising gifts of playful smiles.

Flowery smells on her Norwegian plates.
Both would taste his curry
made with pure orange roasted
Masala spice of the home country
and served with yellow rice and raisins.
Echoes of silent dinners in Kimberley and upset tables.
Silver moonlight beamed on their boyish brown
faces as joy tried to look their way.

she, the sea

shyly, i come to her
and wonder if i will
hear her rhythmic voice
her forceful, distant cry
her brother the sun
comes and goes
drunk with love
wild with or without
women by his side
he laughs at life
and looks jealously at me

but it is she
whom i desire today
her words, eloquent and
silent, spraying me with
their cool, wet touch
stirring my naked body
passionately, secretly, fiery
like young roses our red
lips meet but only when
children look the other way
...no one will see us, *non*

i am hers
even for one day
though her
misty eyes stray away
and beckon others
the wind, her mother, smiles
breezingly at me: "you must
give her seed—not sorrow
to flower her garden of delight
and only then will she
be your wife, by moon's light."

the seduction of Desire

his hot lips were quickly covered in her thick rouged wet lips; she beamed, eyes wide open,
legs soft as the sea and brown as the sand came to his tender touch; the poet's writing hand

stroked her silky black hair this night—it felt good, or so her body said so; her mound didn't
want sweet pats, though his fingers soon searched there; this, on a busy church street and after,

their dance of passion came alive; men looked curiously at two strangers who could not see them
while she sat closely beside him as his young wife, as crowds poured through, as night dreamed;

"diamonds are for love and rubies are for passion," said she smilingly like daddy's happy
frustrated girl, and he eyed her ring of friendship and showed her his, only for her to see it on his

wedding finger; a silent question from her, another feel of her hungry inner legs by him; dolphins
called them both after the lunar eclipse; now he held her gently and the taste of this unusual

flower was too exotic to leave, breasts becoming buds in her mouth the night before; love, she
believed, did not happen and the poet whose words usually flowered seemed silent tonight,

yet his lips were elsewhere, hands working fast as fire; her dark nipples like india's eyes, now
exposed to him, to his innocent bites; her black thong removed revealing a hairless goddess

groove on his soft seabed; bodies flowing first as two, then one, two, then one—tossing, rocking
gently, slowly fast, passionately; kisses, more kisses, many kisses; her foamy wetness became the

sea's shush turning to fields of flowery joy; her womanly perfume a sensual infatuation; clitoral
wishes now excited cries and more cries, then turning to soft, slow whispers; ample brown hips

bucked against his hard hardness, harder than he thought he could past 2 a.m.; silence slept
at dawn as waves retreated after the sound of their voices collided like the succulent surf

against the rigid rock at life's untreaded shoreline; and so in his mind, he penned Desire a poem
but she didn't even know it, she didn't even feel it; her calls remained silent many days

after yet he still felt her with his dark flaming eyes and bare hands night after endless night.

in this place i love you

for daisuke

in this place, with its green sea breeze
and long, long beaches, holding smells
and sights of your sleek perfumed brown body
i love you.

the wind and earth are your loving parents
the water and sun are mine; they know each
other like friends, and from day to day, visit.
mi amor, i mourn for you always.

it was the water that brought us
together. i was closest to my mother's
deep, deep body and you stood next
to me but not beside me. you were too afraid.
was it me or the darkness of the sea?

in this place, i love you.
here, touch it, feel it as i, you.
my burning body, stroked by the
sun's red-hot hands, is inscribed with
my simple, silent words. i am too
afraid to speak them to you. i only want to touch
your lips, *si.* to hear the stories of your people.

but in this place, i love you.
i can mouth what i want to say to you softly.
as gentle as your mother's brave hands
which fitted neatly into mine, foldingly.
in this place i love you.

naked like the sun

streams of breath, sea-blue
paint and sweep over me,
my raging brown body is
black with love, hot with dark desire
the colour of africa, i sweat blue-green
wet dreams into the ice-cold sea

amor inolvidable (unforgettable love)

she still sounds like him
soft, hard, soft, hard
receding into distant memory
the everyday sultry sound
his tongue and pure red heart pounding
like the far drum beats of his people
his hot hands and cool lips colliding
finding one another, still searching, *si*
like the unknown sun on the shrinking shore
our endless beach that shelters us from life's
raging storm ... water and full moons make
hearts bleed over and over again like crashing waves
bringing in tides of gentle young rose petals washing ashore

black man walking

black as the burning sun
black as hard coal, as no one
he strides like an unbreakable
one-hundred-metre sprinter
the race has not yet begun
lone lit cigarette swaying in clenched hand
waiting for thirsty, distant lips
he thinks, then smokes
like he wants no one to fuck with him
white men look hungrily
yet he is the solitary island today naked
alone, silent, shoeless, drifting shoreless
only to search the remote waves of life
still dreaming of home, and love.

water to sun, sea to shore

that black chinese tattoo ... see it high, poised like a passionate mark of love and pain
on my swimmer's strong shoulder, my lanky writing arm, guarding me, part of me
you smiled into my eyes, my red-hot veins, my waters quenched your thirsty lips
your waves swept over my boy's eyes and your silent stormy sea
laughed out loud playing with me softly, softly, softly, *si mi vida*

sinful kisses like seven simple songs, kisses like seven simple songs
filled with roses, and your people's rhythms and rhymes
and passionate brushes of your ancient body on my aching lips
the colour of an angry sun, the taste of sea-green breezes licking me
i nestled close with you on our cheap but warm blanket, its brilliant hue exploding like

plants, trees and water coming alive with the colour of bright, new unexpected affection
love was our ravenous dance, high above in forested mountains
love was like the beat of the rough pacific ocean waves, with you riding atop
the surging crest, taking a chance beside me as if we were going
to die the next day; waves thrashing, washing, cleansing, calming

palm leaves sheltering us, cradling us and veiled mosquito net draping our
bed of passion, still young and gentle as our touch; a cold stone shower held
our burnt brown bodies, entwined, pulsating like the sea, like us knowing and
becoming her sound, her glory, her fury as we rocked to sleep, blazing arm in arm
the glowing candle of light that lit my delicate hand's way—to think, to love, write and speak

deeply of this fragile earth, this last night of our century, your people and mine
"mi casa es tu casa," you reminded me as winds led our way to climb through swirling heat
and blackflies to push forward to water gently falling from high above, it spraying us lightly
as we watched two young boys descend on soft, innocent white sands as they playfully urged
hundreds of ivory white pelicans to fly from a shallow lagoon and make their way home

> *si mi amor, si mi vida, mi corazón,* i long for your dark gentle brown eyes
> eyes that spoke my only name, my name, their delicacy, the sea's soft breeze holds
> me like my mother and i can feel you swaying me, swaying me, singing to me, *si*
> like young dolphins swimming in love and the heat of your sunny shore
> makes me sleepy hot with liquid blue dreams, dreams of love's deep wounds
> like a guitar weeping in the wind, like a guitar weeping in the wind

he speaks to me in silent tones

oceans
have always
told me that
love is on the
other side

two incomes
are better than one
but love can be lonely
if not too poor

i told you
about my
shattered self
with a smile
let you into my

different world
we spoke the same
language, you were the
first to really hear me
if by fate our hearts

collided, i couldn't stop
imaginging you; i wanted us
to go out and play, left to write back
even telephone, leaving desperate calls
but then you cut me off

like a sharp knife,
blood still
drippppppping wet
...young love bleeds too easily
and remembers
tenderness soon missed
soon left to wash out to sea, drifting alone

he catches beautiful butterflies

he catches beautiful butterflies
at the september shore of life
that flutter to him in the cool breeze
that float to him to his tanned, sun-dried feet
and away from him again like a dancing partner
stepping away on toes along the shrinking sleepy shore
with sprinkles of sea rocks, lonely feathers and shells stirred by
life's echoes scattered about

he catches beautiful butterflies
and stands there listening to
the shushy flutter of the ocean's chanting call, its longing like his
there, where he watched the world go by
there, where his life came back to him, floated by
wind blowing on the cool, hot sand
they, charcoal-black and orange-tipped winged doves, beautiful messages
like brown-skinned women, come close by
there where his life came back to him, floated by
she smiles like a seventies love child, sunny flowers in her fro
as she rises from golden water and lathers sun lotion on his
smooth swimmer's back that he cannot reach
she smiles, he dreams, dreams and paints and paints
her penny-shaped nipples kiss him tenderly
her weaves of worn-up hair hold the people's stories like an african goddess
and blankets over him cosily as he sleeps like a shy seven–year-old
floating to him, floating to him
'round and 'round and 'round
like a lustrous black pearl, she opens
shiny and wet, shiny and wet
like the sea's shimmering clitoris
she urges him to wait for her, to come for her and hold her
as she flies and flies and flies
across the naked skins of unhurried men who have seen the world
across the naked shores of life, his deep pool of lonely desire
as they hover above stone and shell, treaded by distant lovers

he catches beautiful butterflies
and smiles gladly as he looks over ancient waves
music too beautiful to hold
breathing in his mother's mysterious ways

jumbo empanadas

An old dark blue Ford station wagon parked on the busy road holds two boys who speak the language of their friendly distant island, sleeping children who are overcome with heat in prams, the lone buzzing hornet landing on my spicy-hot food, blinding bright sunlight beaming on my burning hand as it guides its way across my white page full of messy memories, the black graffiti of yesterday painted on a nearby wall and the rich quilt of many people talking, smiling, shopping for meats, vegetables and fresh fruit sweet with taste. This is the place they journey to excitedly. The place they live. This is all life. All living, breathing, moving in a delicate dance that takes place like an unfinished tapestry of incredible beauty each weekend. Time means nothing for those travelling in these cosmic spaces where people, cultures and ideas merge as one moving vibrant stream.

Coats heavy with yesterday's warmth selling for a pittance and a smile hang outside across the road on Augusta Avenue. A boy, both innocent and young with life, slides the little of his hand into a box of beans on the swamped street that look at him playfully and tauntingly. And now he bashfully and casually comes closer to his mother who speaks to a woman-friend, and goes back to feel the hard smooth roundness of each pinto bean, skin spotted in colour and calling out his lovely name. These are more than magic to him. These represent playful dreams, dreams in which he smiles with life as his soft brown eyes look at me wonderingly, then quickly shy away like playful love.

on my warm bed

can i enter your blk wurld
your infinite universe
and soft sea bed of sweet liquid
smiles—oozing sighs
i dive for your lustrous pearl,
shiny, sweet, soft, smooth
cinnamon thighs
my passionate wurds, gurl
wrap around your delicate,
warm body of depth
hard, soft, strong
as you let go of everything that hurt
you deep inside
all that made you
afraid of life
death, love
you are around me in a
semi-circle like mother nature—life
so beautiful, so divine
that i want to kiss you softly, soulfully forever
sing you love poems, dripping wet with my desire
we are entwined forever and ever in love's sea
its mossy green and exploding shiny violet,
its driftwood
and laughing sky blue is our gentle
breath, our joy, our world
where sarah vaughan's melodies glow and flow
through us like a silent shiver
and the word *amour*
sounds to us like a child's quiet and beautiful silly love song
swinging from here to there quickly,
floating effortlessly back again
leaving our lips breathless
and painted rouge red and moist
with the innocent fragrance of the soft white of young roses

naked / truth

bare to the shore
and sea
i can
be naked
in front
of you
utterly exposed to
your desperate truth
yet penniless
penless
without
any of my
most loved
possessions
no longer
standing in front of
my floor mirror
looking at my self, alone
alone in four separate ways
and distant directions
i am
what i was
yesterday
and centuries ago
—my bed of passion
pierces my heart and
is without warmth,
too small and empty
i cannot lie ... without you
my uncovered, unwashed body
hides no shame
though guilt is nameless
yet spineless and too painful
i am   open
laying breathlessly hot and black
like the beach's soft sand
waiting for you
to catch
me falling submerged
again within your tender arms

100 kisses at twenty

she is needy and
soft as spring's last snow
hot and spicy
black with love
summery heat flowing
through sweat filled with ecstasy
through sweet, untamed hip hop grooves
that captured my wild, shirtless moves
eyes—eyes that wished desirously
eyes and feeling hands that imagined
her beside me as we speak
those rosy lips i dared to kiss sneakfully
those delicate hands that
have known men's hungry
selfish ways and angry wars
wanted sweet, sweet hugs now
"you bite, you bite,
...slower, and gentle," i heard
from her and then said all right
only to take her into my craving arms,
her ancestors knew the bitter
pain of hatred, the shackles of
slavery in a place called
home and exile where
saltwater spirituals were sung
—the mixing of black with
french blood: mad, secret passion
my steamy body envelopes her
slim round hips gently like brushstrokes
her warm tongue touches my light lips like
the sea's breath only for her to come closer
slippery as pisces, playful and wet with heat
...both of us want love i think
and she feels my passionate eyes
as fierce as fire, as sunny life
as she grinds into me, hot skin to skin
my hands and wooing words glide over
her veiled womanhood
soft with feel, virginal and vulnerable
with innocence and rapturous beauty.

if i should lose you

when nina moans, blue as black, blue as black   blue
she knows what the world wants, yearns for
i weep, i weep, feel low-down, and lie silently alone
like christ just before the last supper
i know her; i want to call him—the lover of truth and men,
i desperately want to call him
but there are rivers of books, rivers of books—words, unspoken
lives coming apart like the spines of volumes on love
caresses too afraid between us
i cannot swim to him with my eyes closed even in cold, murky waters
waters so bluish black that nina sounds like another pop star
i have to listen, listen to each one of her sssssssstretching notes
each last cry to understand how naked my lost love is
nina haunts me and sometimes i have to run and hide
for i fear for my poor black child's heart, for we have known the same
soft, shameful melody, we have danced to it alone many a night, the last
to leave the hot dark nightclub, half drunk and sweating with lust on our lips
we have danced holding ourselves alone, too long, too long
nina calls me out to play again, but i say no

mummy calls me home and she hums sweetly as breakfast smells beautiful

rivers of red flames

fire and water do not mix, fire and water do not mix as night turns to day
for he cannot swim; waves make him panic and edgy and he stands alone at the far shore

yet he is drawn to my soaring and soothing waves, wickedly though playfully
life's gentle song can be forgotten by some, though not all can sing too well as a duo

his waters run too wild and few have seen him without clothes and silent as the threatening sky
what of close dear friendship or boyhood days and mischief; with tired, pleasant smiles

we always share the same sweet drink in two ice-filled glasses at the same stale bar,
sitting alone or with the smiling tanned dancer whose hands washed his mother's dying body;

our fathers, we thought were invicible with life but their death may be the end of innocence
and the birth of manhood, creeping up and withering us down like summer's surprizing storms

beside me, he walks as the famed unknown actor in many a silent film; he is strong and i
fear his still, explosive storms while i am the unread love poem yet too fragile without him

the wind blows and howls over years of lovelessness, only to mourn, only to wait endlessly
our lips do not touch, they do not—*non*, yet they secretly want to speak, retell

the same beautiful songs that we cannot sing to each other yet, that we cannot mouth
life moves on too quickly and his paintings do not sell well, making for sleepness nights

in which sweet dreams turn to unfamiliar afraid darkness; he wants his young looks back again
and desires my arm in the black of night, moon upon us; i gently take his arm and then we speak

as two, as two and as one; i see a bit of short grey hair washing down my sink; age is not
kind to desperate, lonely men; the heart is silent, it does not weep, it is only silent

poetry is cheap like porn and bad sex and my words are too wintry and viciously cold
now he wants a barking child by august and between life's pages, i'll maybe babysit

is this to be our lovely meaning, or will my fingers touch buds, even plant seeds that swim
up warm rivers, bringing forth new life for me to relive my innocent childhood, even his again?

he lay there nakedly, floating and listening at the edge of life, hands spread out like christ

let this cleanse u
breathe, breathe...
let this sun
circling the wide, wide
wondrous sky and blue
its sultry setting so close yet distant
as a child's petalled hand
cleanse u
breathe, breathe...
and the wind's gentle breath
draping u   take that, too
take it all in, take it like
u've just ran forever
and ever
let my eyes be the endless sea
and my crazy lips touch your body blue
like the taste of home—sweetbread
let this calm, cool water
dripping, laying quietly,
pouring,
taste, smell and exalt in it
feel its liquid summery love
let it be part of u
all of it, forever
take the wooden hollow cup filled
as the ocean's awaiting bashful breeze
take it all in like your mother's baked cake
filled with creamy delight
and float, float up, eyes, up
as u would my love, take it
my sculptor's working, waiting hand   *open*

love's poverty

all i have to give is my heart
my pockets are empty of words
i bought him a soft pink dolphin and he left
me standing there silently at the airport
the tributaries of my heart, bruised
like trust cut and incarcerated away
like rivers, dry as my throat
tears flow, tears flow, hands bloodied by the past
with the memory of time
i quench for the sweet taste
of his kiss, red wine's smooth passion
honey is water to some
and love escapes a
daughterless mother and fades to dust

all i have to give is my heart
brown skinned, brown thing
ashamed, the sizzling summer's sun calling my name
the water shining like blue gold on me
seven seas call sleep, peace and darkness
Moon, Sun, sea and sky are the poet's love signs
mi amor leaves like a desperate man who mistook me
for a wealthy gringo—but money cannot buy love
and love is simple, beautiful—not fit, attractive or rich
my soul is the entrance to Her watery world
i am lonely and she, silent, crushed like the Earth
knives know pain and sanity is unbearable
all i have to give is my heart, all, all.

with this ring, i thee wed

a love poem did not flow through his silent and sleepy fingers, for they
only pondered early the next morning over strong coffee at 6 a.m.; feelings—uncertain
and unsure—flowered for isn't that what the language of the heart is all about?

and he remembered an island man, his hair worn tight as a tree's roots, whose luck was
born on the blessed day's rest, who had given up on sex and love, who professed:
"if a man does not lie with you, he treats you with a bit of dignity and respect!"

his eyes dark aflame and a flat wide nose was the poet's, only larger,
his manhood darker, imposing, curved, struck the cold air like lightning; black hands held
coloured hands and coloured hands held black hands momentarily: history's retold story

the weaver of hair undressed himself for Love that night while the penniless poet writes
again as rain falls to drench his tired pen, to soak his mood caressing him love astray, water
dripping softly like tears as al green and marvin gaye sing amour soulfully;

he met him earlier groovin in sexy black hip briefs to silently mouth to him: "tell me, what do
your hands make," without even knowing this brotha or holding him tenderly; a lucky silver
ring of kissing dolphins swam on the wedding finger of one while the other stood smiling

and so now fond memories of floating drenched on a feather down bed with
indian silk pillows, return gently; the strangeness of the summer's hot, tired night had
given way to a smooth wave, a gentle quiet wave; it flowed like a painter's delicate hand

that lightly trailed across the rise of a firm torso towards the crashing soft crest
of a lower back—a deep, breathless, beautiful gully—and made its way to two high
sloping midnight mossy mountains and finally to flowery moist lips

lips, that sang fiery songs of the heart

that whispered love's hidden secrets, some too painful, others smiling
unlike the poet's warm tears of intense longing.

the long night

Love longs so much that it finds its name in the story of a black poet speaking his truth and on the lips of an exiled dancer—the youngest son of Jews—who has dared to escape and rid himself of Israel. His nation's sins and the horror of war are revealed each day: two young children, Arabs, were killed by the army yesterday. And a settler's infant boy does not breathe, a bullet piercing his innocent, delicate heart. "I have heard you can trust someone when they kiss you and look you straight in the eye," the dancer said to the poet as they lay together in each other's arms revelling in the sweetness of their caresses, the night soon giving way to the day's heat. A full yellow moon followed them home, calling the young one who did not want to take a shower at first, not wanting pity. "I have to go pee!" exclaimed the poet, waiting anxiously and knocking on the locked bathroom door as the younger one finally showered forever and ever. Hot water fell on him over his worn body, bruised with hunger and exhaustion. It made him want to return home to his mother's loving arms. And only after several minutes, the water still running, was the poet let in. But his young friend exclaimed, "Oh, don't come in the shower just yet!" Much later the door was opened, steam rising. Heat pulsating.

He walked out quietly and nonchalantly, a wet gold towel wrapped tightly around his slim waist, hiding his lean body that knew pain and had been close to death many years ago. Alone and uncertain as the night, his life was as complex and old as the sea that he crossed perilously. Only kisses, kisses of simple soft beauty could unwrap him and his troubles. Their bloodied circumcisions, the memory of their fathers, mingled and touched now. And lonely lips soon greeted them as sons of torn nations. Nations afraid and armed, unsure of peace. Unadorned letters of love remained in their minds and were left the next morning for each had awoken with hearts lit aflame.

meal-ha-ma / shalom (war / peace)

for joav

i
knew
mordecai
for i, too,
have loved
a jew yet
fled love
and its
desperate
arms as they
pulled me straight in the defenceless eyes of a destitute man
his young
traitor's
heart
on fire
his soft
and wet
hands
punctured
with the
deep
bloody
wounds
of senseless
war
hebrew
against
arab
arab
against
jew
"forgive me
israel,"
he begs,
"forgive me."

the question

"Why do you think our lonely hearts met?" I asked him tenderly as he sat on the flowery futon, half-dressed and anxious. "I understand suffering. Why do you think my family left South Africa? And my mother stayed behind because of my father? She and her family remained there without money and meals. And the four children lived and died in Canada without her. And then when I returned to bury her that was my life staring at me there in the heavy coffin in Johannesburg, the fathomless cold earth hugging and holding her. That was all of my life summed up in one second, one picture..." He quickly got up, put his faded jeans, peace T-shirt and my old dock shoes on and stood silently on the bare balcony outside, a pigeon sitting there, to light up an anxious smoke. He wanted his big beige winter hat as his head felt the cool air even though this was May. And he looked out into the unknown distance silently with frightened eyes, the city's faceless skyscrapers nearly touching him. Tears held back, he thought of home. Our love music was playing inside with booming horns and her smooth sassy voice reminding us of each other again.

love / death

I cannot let go of love or its tempting smell and exquisite taste.
I paint it, so that my coloured fingers are smudged in its rouge richness. A gentle reminder.

If I do not hold onto the anguished brush of my heart, my canvas, my only portrait
of him will perish, like my mother's desperate and delicate hand. My father is buried at

the foot of his father's tired feet. Will I return to my mother's waiting arms or find another?
Her hand slips away from my child's silent hand at the airport, drums beating mournfully over

incoming tides. Young flower petals moist with the wetness of dreams do not brush my thirsty
lips now. Only falling tears—memory.

About the Author

Norman G. Kester was born in Kimberley, South Africa, and emigrated with his family to Canada in 1969. His hardworking father soon followed his uncle and their family when grand apartheid was introduced in the Republic. Mr. Kester is the editor of the ground-breaking *Liberating Minds* and recently authored *From here to District Six: a South African memoir*. He has also written a radio play and short fiction, and his work has been published in Canada, the United States and South Africa. A member of the League of Canadian Poets and the Liaison of Independent Filmmakers of Toronto, he has taught creative writing workshops in libraries and worked as a librarian. Mr. Kester has been a long-serving and active member of the Canadian Book and Periodical Council's Freedom of Expression Committee. He resides in Toronto.

Acknowledgements

Thanks to poet and writing instructor David Donnell and my enthusiastic classmates in the Master Class in Poetry at the University of Toronto who gave me insightful suggestions in revising versions of my manuscript. Further appreciation should also be extended in this regard to humanities scholar Rinaldo Walcott and especially to English scholar and friend Rozena Maart, who has been a great source of emotional and intellectual support over the years where there was little, and whose own work in social justice and post-colonial thought and literature through the Biko Institute makes my literary work and activism that more urgent. Additional praise to poet-playwright andra simons, in Bermuda, for supporting my writing and to painter Manuel Palacio for allowing me to make use of "Wedding Belle." Tania–*gracias* for the revealing photographs you carefully crafted of Kensington Market where my pen guides my spirit. Without copy editor and proofreader Elizabeth Phinney, this book would never have reached its final version. A sincere note of appreciation to Jim Drake and, finally, to Brian Lam, who worked diligently in designing the striking cover art for *Liquid love and other longings*. And thank you to my loving sisters and niece who teach me something innately beautiful each day. I am but a lone branch without their nurturing roots of support and wisdom.